Generational Wealth

Creating a Family Legacy

Table of Contents

Chapter 1. Introduction

Welcome to this comprehensive Special Report on Generational Wealth: Creating a Family Legacy. This engaging resource promises to be your step-by-step guide in navigating the exciting journey of securing your family's financial future across generations. No longer a privilege reserved for only the elite, amassing generational wealth is within everyone's reach, and this illuminating report will show you exactly how! You will discover sound strategies, unique perspectives, and practical advice on wealth accumulation, management, and transfer, all wrapped in an easily understandable format. Embark on this empowering journey today, and let your family's legacy radiate financial stability and prosperity for generations to come!

Chapter 2. Understanding Generational Wealth

The concept of generational wealth might seem complex at first glance, encased in financial jargon and intricate monetary mechanisms. However, once you unravel the mystery behind its crucial components, you begin to understand that generational wealth is not an inaccessible goal, but rather a tangible target. It's about creating a legacy — a financial footprint that will enable successive generations to thrive without experiencing severe monetary constraints.

2.1. Defining Generational Wealth

Generational wealth, or legacy wealth, is the wealth a person accrues over his or her lifetime and passes down to future generations. This amassed wealth takes various forms — monetary assets, real estate, stocks and bonds, fine arts, a successful business, and more. The ability to sustain wealth generation after generation is what differentiates generational wealth from individual wealth.

The multiple forms that generational wealth encompasses make it flexible and adaptable to your financial situation and goals. The first step to acquiring generational wealth is understanding and determining the form that is most suitable for your wealth creation strategy.

2.2. Components of Generational Wealth

The creation of generational wealth draws upon three primary components: wealth accumulation, wealth preservation, and wealth transfer. A comprehensive understanding of these elements sets the foundation for planning and implementing generational wealth strategies.

- **Wealth accumulation** refers to the act of amassing assets or capital that holds or increases in value over time. This accumulation occurs through consistent savings, prudent investments, or successful entrepreneurship.

- **Wealth preservation**, on the other hand, focuses on protecting the amassed wealth from losses due to market fluctuations, inflation, or ill-advised financial decisions. This involves adopting sound financial risk management practices and a well-diversified investment portfolio.

- Lastly, **wealth transfer** involves the distribution of accumulated wealth to future generations. This step focuses on crafting effective estate plans or trusts that prepare for smooth wealth transition in the event of your death or incapacitation.

Each of these components requires an intimate knowledge of diverse financial concepts and techniques. However, the study and application of these ideas is within everyone's reach with the right information and dedication.

2.3. Accumulating Wealth

Saving is the first step towards wealth accumulation. The process involves setting aside a portion of one's income regularly, focusing on living within one's means, and reducing frivolous spending. While the process may be slow, over time, the results can be substantial.

On the other hand, investments offer a faster route to wealth accumulation. Investments in stocks, bonds, or real estate can grow your wealth exponentially over time if managed well.

Lastly, entrepreneurship has the potential to generate significant wealth. Building a successful business not only provides you with a steady income stream, but it also opens opportunities for creating jobs, increasing your wealth, and securing your family's financial stability.

While these three pathways to wealth accumulation vary in risk and reward, effective use of a combination can lead to substantial wealth creation.

2.4. Preserving Wealth

Once wealth is amassed, it's equally important to preserve it. Wealth preservation strategies include diversification of investments, hedging against inflation and market volatility through safe assets like treasury bonds, and securing comprehensive insurance coverage.

Another crucial wealth preservation strategy involves sound tax planning. Understand legislation around tax-imposed wealth in order to deploy strategies that minimize its impact while staying within legal boundaries.

2.5. Transferring Wealth

Wealth, once accumulated and preserved, must eventually be transferred to future generations. Effective wealth transfer mechanism can minimize tax obligations, avoid probate and family disputes, and assure the continuation of your financial legacy.

Planning for wealth transfer involves decisions about wills, trusts, and estate plans, which can get complex depending on the size and nature of your wealth. It's advisable to consult with experts such as estate planning attorneys or financial advisors to guide you through the process.

In conclusion, generational wealth offers an effective solution for financial independence, not just for you, but for generations to come. Grasping the three central components – accumulation, preservation, and transfer of wealth – is essential in creating a lasting legacy. With time, dedication, and careful financial navigation, generational wealth becomes not just a dream, but an attainable reality.

Chapter 3. The Psychology Behind Money and Wealth Creation

To truly understand wealth creation, it is crucial to delve into the psychological underpinnings. Unraveling our deep-rooted conceptions about money, and the behaviors these notions elicit, paves the way for attaining and preserving wealth.

3.1. Money Beliefs and Emotions

We are not born with money beliefs, but they develop over time, influenced heavily by our parents, caregivers, or the environment we grow up in. These deeply ingrained money beliefs have the power to shape our financial decisions in significant ways, often unconsciously. Dissecting these beliefs is the first step toward allowing for well-informed, deliberate decisions about generational wealth building.

However, our relationship with money isn't solely cognitive. In fact, money frequently stirs strong emotions—joy, anxiety, insecurity, or relief—that influence our financial behavior. Learning to identify and cope with these emotions is vital in order to avert behaviors that may hinder wealth accumulation.

3.2. Financial Behaviors

Our financial behaviors, heavily influenced by our money beliefs and emotions, play a definitive role in wealth creation. These habits include our propensity to save or spend, our investment strategies, and our ability to balance short-term and long-term financial goals. Nurturing financially beneficial habits is a cornerstone of building generational wealth.

3.3. The Habit of Saving

One of the most fundamental financial habits is saving. Understanding the psychology behind saving not only helps to set realistic saving goals but also aids in seeking effective techniques to meet these goals. Automatic saving plans, for example, force us to 'pay ourselves first' by saving a portion of our income before it gets spent.

3.4. Cognitive Biases and Money Decisions

Cognitive biases are systematic errors in thinking that significantly affect our decisions and judgments. Numerous biases impact our financial decisions, including the confirmation bias (preferring information that confirms pre-existing beliefs) and recency bias (prioritizing recent occurrences over historic ones). By regularly scrutinizing our financial decisions, we can begin to observe and correct these biases.

3.5. Money and Self-worth

Another psychological factor that influences wealth creation is the association between money and self-worth. People often equate wealth with success, leading to a pursuit of money for the wrong reasons. Recognizing the difference between external symbols of wealth and genuine financial security is critical.

3.6. The Need for Financial Literacy

Financial literacy—the understanding of various financial areas, including managing personal finances, money and investing, and preparing for retirement—is a key component in wealth creation. The low levels of financial literacy across many demographics highlight the necessity for finance education as a tool to foster wealth-building behaviors.

3.7. Financial Psychology and Generational Wealth

Financial psychology provides insights into the mutual influence of money and human behavior. This knowledge can be harnessed to cultivate behaviors and beliefs conducive to generational wealth creation. Our financial behaviors, shaped by our psychological relationship with money, have a lasting impact, shaping not just our own wealth but also that which we pass down to future generations.

3.8. Overcoming Psychological Barriers

Understanding the psychology behind wealth creation also means recognizing the psychological barriers that inhibit it. These barriers can manifest as self-limiting beliefs ("I'm not good with money"), procrastination on financial planning, or a harmful scarcity mindset. Overcoming these obstacles necessitates confronting our unhealthy money beliefs and transforming them into empowering ones.

3.9. Money Mindset Transformation

Building generational wealth isn't just about accumulating wealth but changing how we perceive and handle money. This transformation requires developing a healthy money mindset—one that appreciates the value of money as a tool for security and prosperity, rather than an end in itself. This shift in perception paves the way towards financial habits that are sustainable across generations.

3.10. Conclusion

Understanding the psychology behind money and wealth creation is crucial to building generational wealth. Our money beliefs and behaviors, shaped by a myriad of psychological factors, determine our financial practice. Harnessing this knowledge allows us to develop healthy financial habits, overcome psychological barriers, and transform our money mindset, setting up a legacy of wealth that transcends generations.

Chapter 4. Principles of Personal Finance and Wealth Accumulation

To ensure a stable and prosperous financial future for your family, understanding the principles of personal finance and wealth accumulation is key. Whether you aim for global recognition, a peaceful retirement, or creating a lasting legacy, it all begins with mastering the principles outlined in this section of this report.

4.1. Understanding Personal Finance

Personal finance pertains to how individuals and families budget, save, and spend their money, taking into consideration various financial risks and future life events. By understanding personal finance, you are in a better position to meet your individual needs and financial goals.

When planning personal finance, consider the following areas:

- Income: The amount you earn from your occupation and other sources

- Budget: How you plan your income to manage your financial life

- Savings: The portion of your income that you save for future use

- Expenses: The money you spend on your needs and wants

- Investments: Your plan for growing your wealth by committing capital in order to gain profitable returns

Through diligent planning and regular reviews, you can ensure your financial well-being across your lifetime.

4.2. The Importance of Budgeting

Budgeting is a cornerstone of personal finance. By creating and sticking to a budget, you establish a roadmap for financial success.

Budgeting helps with:

- Spending patterns: A budget provides a clear overview of how you're spending money, enabling you to reduce unnecessary expenses.

- Focusing on financial goals: By earmarking income for the future, your budget keeps you firmly on the path to achieving your financial objectives.

- Saving for emergencies: A budget ensures that you allocate money towards an emergency fund, providing a safety net for unexpected costs.

- Planning for retirement: With a budget, you can consistently set aside money for life after work.

Remember, a budget is a living operation, so it's essential to review and adjust it periodically to incorporate changes in income, expenses, and financial goals.

4.3. Saving and Investing

Saving and investing are key principles in personal finance and wealth accumulation.

- Saving: Money put aside in a secure place like a savings account, which offers moderate but guaranteed returns. It ensures you have funds for emergencies or short-term financial goals.

- Investing: Money allocated for purchasing assets (e.g., stocks, bonds, or real estate) that have the potential for a higher return, albeit with higher risk. Investment helps grow wealth over the long term.

Both strategies should coexist in your personal finance plan. Savings cater to security, while investments build your wealth.

4.4. Debt Management

Debt is not inherently bad. Managed wisely, it can help you achieve life goals, such as home ownership or higher education. However, excessive or poorly managed debt can lead to financial distress.

Key tips for debt management include:

- Borrow only what you can afford to repay

- Shop around for the lowest interest rates

- Pay your bills on time to avoid late fees and protect your credit score

- Make extra payments when possible to reduce the total interest paid

4.5. Insurance and Risk Management

Insurance is your financial shield against unforeseen circumstances. From health issues to car accidents, insurance helps you mitigate the financial impact of emergencies.

Here's what to consider:

- Life insurance: Protects your dependents in case of your untimely demise

- Health insurance: Covers medical expenses

- Disability insurance: Provides income if you're unable to work due to disability

- Homeowners/Renters insurance: Protects you against damage to your home or its contents

- Auto insurance: Covers damages caused by car accidents

Remember, insurance is about managing risk. Evaluate potential scenarios and invest in appropriate insurance coverage.

4.6. Retirement Planning

Retirement planning is a significant component of personal finance. It enables a comfortable life post-employment. The earlier you start, the more time your money has to grow.

Key aspects of retirement planning include:

- Understanding retirement costs: Take into account expected expenses like healthcare costs, living expenses, travel, and hobbies.

- Using tax-efficient retirement savings accounts: Leverage retirement savings accounts like 401(k)s or Individual Retirement Accounts (IRAs) that offer tax benefits.

- Diversifying investments: Mitigate risk by spreading your money across various types of investments.

- Factoring in Social Security: This may provide a portion of your retirement income.

- Reviewing and adjusting your retirement plan: As you age, your financial situation, risk tolerance, and goals will change. Regular adjustments ensure that your retirement plan stays aligned with your needs.

With this understanding of personal finance and wealth accumulation, you are well on your way to securing a prosperous future for your family. Keep these principles in mind as you continue the journey towards generational wealth.

Chapter 5. The Power of Compounding Interest

Compounding interest, often referred to as the eighth wonder of the world, is one of the most powerful tools available for wealth creation. It is a simple, yet remarkable concept that manifests the power of time when it comes to investments. At first glance, it may seem underwhelming, but its beauty lies in its effects over long periods, turning even modest savings into hefty amounts.

5.1. Understanding Compounding Interest

Compounding interest can be understood as 'interest on interest'. It means that you earn interest not only on the initial amount (the principal) you invested but also on the interest that your investment has already earned. This results in your money growing at an increasing rate, hence building wealth over time.

Let's consider a simple example to illustrate the power of compounding. Suppose you invest $1000 at an annual interest rate of 5%. If the interest is compounded annually, after the first year, you would have $1050. The original sum of money had increased by $50 due to interest earned. In the second year, you earn interest of 5% not only on the initial $1000 but also on the $50 interest earned in the first year, making your total $1102.5 by the end of the second year. As this process repeats, your wealth grows more rapidly as time moves ahead.

5.2. Frequency of Compounding

The frequency of compounding plays an essential role in

determining the amount of wealth you accumulate. Interest can be compounded annually, semi-annually, quarterly, monthly, or even daily. Generally, the more frequently interest is compounded, the more wealth you amass.

An important term here is the Annual Percentage Yield (APY), also known as effective annual rate (EAR), which refers to the real rate of return earned in a year, considering the effect of compounding interest.

To calculate APY, you can use the formula:

APY = (1 + r/n) ^ (n*t) - 1

where: * r is the annual interest rate (decimal) * n represents the number of compounding periods per year, and * t is the time the money is invested or borrowed for, in years.

The powerful effect of increasing compounding frequency can be illustrated by revisiting our earlier example, this time with quarterly compounding. The $1000 invested at 5% per annum would amount to $1104.89 at the end of two years, as against $1102.5 with annual compounding.

Understandably, the effect of compounding frequency is even more remarkable with more extended investment periods.

5.3. The Time Value of Money

Underpinning the power of compounding is the concept of the time value of money—the notion that money available today is worth more than the same amount in the future due to its potential earning capacity. This core principle of finance holds that, given money can earn interest, any amount of money is worth more the sooner it is received. In the context of compounding, it asserts that the longer you allow your investments to earn and compound interest, the faster your wealth grows.

5.4. Compounding: A Long-Term Strategy

For compounding to work its magic, it needs both time and patience. It's a long-term strategy. The interest you earn in the early years of your investment might seem modest. Yet, as time progresses and the amount on which interest is calculated grows, you begin to see a snowball effect—the growth of your investment accelerates.

For instance, if you start with an investment of $10,000 at an interest rate of 6% compounded annually, in 10 years, your investment would double to about $20,000. In the next 10 years, it grows to about $40,000, and in 10 more years, it's approximately $80,000.

The key takeaway is that it is not just the amount of money but the length of time it's invested that drives wealth creation through compounding.

5.5. Factors Affecting Compounding

There are multiple factors at play influencing the effect of compounding. These include the principal amount, the rate of interest, and the tenure of the investment. In addition, as noted, the frequency of compounding also significantly affects the total return on investment.

By adjusting these levers—investing a more considerable sum, securing a higher rate of interest, extending the investment's tenure, or increasing the frequency of compounding—you can enhance the power of compounding.

5.6. Start Early and Regularly

The most common advice you will hear about compounding is to start early. The sooner you start investing, the more time your money has to grow. This approach leads to a striking outcome: an investor who starts early will often end up with more wealth than someone who starts late, even if the latter invests more money.

On top of starting early, regular investments reinforce the power of compounding. This practice is commonly known as dollar-cost averaging, where you invest a fixed amount of money at regular intervals, regardless of market conditions. Such a consistent approach not only instils financial discipline but also sets the ground for compounding interest to work its magic over time.

In conclusion, harnessing the power of compounding is crucial in building long-lasting generational wealth. With a good understanding of its working, the right strategy, disciplined approach, a patient mindset, and above all, time, you can leverage compounding to create a secure financial legacy for you and your family.

Chapter 6. Real Estate Investment for Generational Wealth

The journey towards generational wealth starts with understanding the available tools and strategies. One such potent instrument is real estate investment. This avenue offers an array of opportunities - from potentially high returns on investment to tax advantages, to an additional income stream.

6.1. Why Real Estate?

Real estate investment is associated with creating wealth across generations for many important reasons – the pivotal being its durable nature. Land and buildings have been appreciated assets for centuries, often increasing in value over time. Unlike tangible possessions that can depreciate and wear down, real estate properties typically appreciate. The adage "They're not making any more land" holds true – the scarcity of real estate, particularly in populous or desirable locations, helps drive its long-term value growth.

Real estate investments can provide steady cash flow in the form of rental income. This is a significant benefit if, for example, one of your revenue streams experiences a setback. It is, in essence, a built-in income diversification strategy.

Moreover, the value of your real estate investment is relatively independent of stock market fluctuations, meaning it can be a safer, more stable option during economic downturns. Although property values can experience decreases, they are generally less volatile than stocks and other investments.

Finally, owning real estate provides substantial tax benefits. These include deductions on mortgage interest, property taxes, and operational expenses, as well as depreciation. Real estate can also provide tax-free income (in certain circumstances) and be an efficient estate planning tool.

6.2. Selecting the Right Investment Property

Choosing the right investment property is a crucial step in your quest for generational wealth through real estate. What constitutes "right" will vary across individuals based on factors like risk tolerance, long term goals, and initial capital outlay.

Look for properties in up-and-coming areas. These locations often have property prices at the lower end of the scale but have excellent potential for future price appreciation. Also, assess the vicinity's economic indicators, such as job growth, new infrastructure, or planned developments, which may positively influence property values.

Perform thorough market research before investing. Understand the rental yield of the property you're considering. High rent can translate into a substantial income stream and recovery of the initial property investment over time.

6.3. Financing Your Real Estate Investment

There are several ways to finance the real estate conditions appropriately to secure a viable deal. Traditional mortgages, hard money loans, private money loans, and real estate wholesaling are such popular strategies to fund your property investment.

Research and understand the benefits and caveats of each. For instance, a traditional mortgage might offer lower interest rates, but qualifying for it might be stringent. Conversely, private money loans offer faster funding and more flexible loan terms, but interest rates can be significantly higher.

6.4. Property Management

Property management is an important aspect of owning rental property, as the level of management can significantly influence the return on your real estate investment. Good property management involves maintaining the property conditions, ensuring rent's timely collection, seeking and retaining good tenants, and complying with relevant rental property laws.

For many investors, property management companies are an excellent choice. They take care of these responsibilities while allowing you to reap the benefits without having to invest the time and effort in day-to-day management.

6.5. Building and Leveraging Equity

Equity refers to the value of the property after all debts (like mortgage) are paid off. As equity increases over time - through property appreciation and mortgage payments – it becomes a leverage tool. You can borrow against it to expand your real estate portfolio or fund other investments - thus exponentially increasing your wealth.

6.6. Conclusion

Real estate investment is a proven avenue to build generational wealth. Its advantages are numerous, from providing a steady income stream to tax savings and leveraging equity. However, like all investments, it comes with associated risks and requires meticulous planning, strategic selection, and effective management. Done wisely, real estate investment can be the key to a prosperous financial future for generations to come.

Chapter 7. Stock Market Mastery and Wealth Creation

The journey to financial prosperity and creating a legacy often rests on diverse investment avenues, ranging from real estate to business ownership, to arguably one of the most lucrative yet often misunderstood – the stock market. This component of the financial world, when correctly understood and astutely managed, could pave the path to sustainable and even exponential wealth for your family.

7.1. Understanding the Stock Market

The stock market is a network of exchanges for trading stocks (shares), commodities, and other financial instruments. Companies list their shares on these exchanges for investors to buy and sell. The stock market is driven by supply and demand dynamics - when there's a larger demand for a company's stock, the price rises. Conversely, when more people want to sell a stock than buy it, the price decreases.

One of the first steps in obtaining stock market mastery is a comprehensive understanding of fundamental analyses. This involves evaluating a company's financials, industry position, and market conditions to determine the stock's intrinsic value.

7.1.1. Fundamentals of Stock Analysis

1. **Income Statement**: Here, you'll find the revenue, expenses, and profit of a company in a given period.

2. **Balance Sheet**: This shows the assets, liabilities, and shareholders' equity, giving a snapshot of a company's financial health.

3. **Cash Flow Statement**: It outlines the company's cash inflows and

outflows and showcases its ability to generate cash.

Keeping an eye on economic indicators like GDP, inflation rates, employment rates, and consumer sentiment can also provide valuable insights into a company's growth potential.

7.2. Crafting a Robust Investment Strategy

In investing, an optimal strategy considers your financial goals, risk tolerance, and investment timeline. You should diversify your portfolio among different company stocks in various industries and even countries to spread and potentially reduce risk.

7.2.1. Long-Term Investing

This involves buying and holding securities with the expectation that they will increase in value over a long period of time. This strategy requires patience, but historically, the stock market trends upwards over extended periods.

7.2.2. Active Trading

Active traders take advantage of short-term price fluctuations. This strategy often involves day trading, swing trading, or scalping. It is recommended only for those who have the time, expertise, and psychological make-up to handle such trades.

7.3. Maximizing Your Returns: Compound Interest and Dividends

Albert Einstein famously described compound interest as the most potent force in the universe. It involves reinvesting earnings (interest, dividends, capital gains) from an investment to grow even more substantial over time.

Dividends provide another smart way to increase your wealth. Certain companies distribute a part of their earnings to shareholders as dividends. Reinvestment of these dividends can further enhance your portfolio value.

7.4. Minimizing Risks: Diversification and Emotion Control

As the saying goes, "Don't put all your eggs in one basket." A diverse portfolio has a mix of different types of assets—stocks, bonds, commodities, real estate—which can help to balance risk.

It's also crucial to invest without letting emotions dictate your actions. The stock market is volatile, but one should avoid selling out of fear during a downturn or buying driven by greed in a market surge. Sticking to your investment plan is crucial.

7.5. Hands-on or Hands-off: Choosing Between Self-Directed and Managed Funds

Should you chase individual stocks or rely on a fund manager's expertise? The answer depends on your knowledge, time availability, and comfort level with managing your own investments.

Self-directed investing provides full control but requires time to research stocks and a knack for analysis. On the other hand, mutual funds or exchange-traded funds (ETFs) offer an easy way to diversify your portfolio and are managed by seasoned professionals.

7.6. Planning for Wealth Transfer

Building generational wealth is not only about accumulating wealth but also effectively transferring it to future generations. An estate plan, a will, and a living trust are some of the tools that can ensure your wealth is passed on seamlessly.

Mastering the stock market and creating wealth is a process that requires education, patience, practice, and strategy. However, once you understand its intricacies, a wealth-generating machine is at your disposal, churning out fortunes that can serve your family for generations. Let this be an insightful and empowering journey to financial freedom and a firm family legacy.

Chapter 8. Effective Estate Planning: Ensuring a Smooth Transition

Effective estate planning is paramount in securing your family's financial health and maintaining harmony among surviving members. It is a legal, orderly process of managing your wealth during your lifetime, and subsequently, distributing it after your demise. If approached strategically, it can successfully mitigate impending disputes and confusion, while also minimizing the taxes and expenses associated with inheritance. Ultimately, it brings you a step closer to leaving a sustainable legacy.

8.1. What is Estate Planning?

Estate planning, at its core, involves making several vital, well-informed decisions about your assets – property, investments, savings, insurance policies, and other personal possessions of value. These decisions will guide the distribution, management, and access to your assets when you are no longer alive, or are unable to make these decisions yourself.

The primary goal of estate planning is to ensure the maximum wealth is distributed to the desired heirs while minimizing the legalities and tax burden. Through this, you safeguard your legacy and provide a roadmap that clearly stipulates the distribution of your wealth, thereby relieving your loved ones from potential conflicts and misunderstandings.

8.2. Components of an Estate Plan

While the specifics might vary based on individual circumstances, an effective estate plan often comprises the following:

- A Will or Testament: It's an indispensable legal document that ensures your assets are distributed per your wishes after your death.

- Power of Attorney (POA): This designates an individual to handle your financial affairs in case you become incapable due to illness or incapacity.

- Beneficiary Designations: Certain assets, such as retirement accounts and life insurance policies, allow you to assign beneficiaries. These designations supersede any instructions laid out in your will.

- Trusts: These are legal mechanisms allowing a third party, the trustee, to hold and manage assets on behalf of the beneficiaries. Trusts could be living (established while you are alive) or testamentary (created through a will after death).

- Letter of Intent: A non-legal document complementing your will or trust, providing additional context or specific wishes.

- Health Care Power of Attorney (HCPOA): Appoints a trusted individual to make critical healthcare decisions on your behalf if you are unavailable or incapable.

- Guardianship Designations: If you have minor or dependent children, it's important to appoint guardians to oversee their wellbeing and finances until they reach adulthood.

Remember, estate planning isn't carved in stone; it should be revisited and revised regularly to mirror significant life changes, such as marriages, divorces, births, deaths, or substantial economic growth or loss.

8.3. The Impact of Taxes on Estate Planning

When it comes to transferring wealth from one generation to the next, taxes can leave a substantial dent. Specifically, estate and inheritance taxes, also referred to as 'death taxes,' can erode your estate's value. Estate taxes are levied on the overall value of the deceased's estate before distribution, while inheritance tax is paid by the recipient on their share.

However, strategic planning can help reduce this tax burden significantly. The use of gifting, trusts, exemptions, and the tax basis step-up in inherited property can be effective at mitigating tax consequences.

Proactive gift giving, for instance, allows you to provide to your heirs while you're alive, reducing the amount that may be subject to estate tax upon death. The IRS allows a certain amount per recipient per year to be gifted tax-free.

Trusts can also be instrumental in tax avoidance. For example, a bypass trust, more formally known as a credit shelter trust, allows you to essentially "double up" on the estate tax exemption.

Finally, the tax basis step-up permits the cost basis of property to be stepped up to its fair market value at the date of the owner's death, potentially escaping a significant capital gain tax upon the sale of the property.

However, the complex nature of tax laws necessitates careful planning and consulting with a tax professional or an experienced attorney.

8.4. The Role of Professionals in Estate Planning

Planning your estate can be a complex matter due to the intricacies and nuances of tax laws, trust creation, and other legal concepts. Moreover, the emotional difficulty of dealing with death and succession can make the process overwhelming. This is where professionals - estate attorneys, financial advisors, tax professionals – can provide guidance.

Estate Attorneys specialize in laws associated with estate planning and can guide in crafting a solid estate plan. They can help you draft legally sound documents like wills, trusts, powers of attorney, and health care directives.

Financial Advisors can provide invaluable insight into squeezing the best returns out of your assets and investments – both while you're still alive and after your death. They can help align your estate plan with your overall financial plan.

Tax Professionals can guide you through the labyrinthine world of tax codes and regulations, assisting in minimizing your estate's tax liability, thus preserving its worth.

These professionals can collaboratively ensure your assets reach your loved ones in the most efficient, stress-free manner possible and your legacy is preserved in the way you've envisioned.

Different professionals have varied competencies, so it's crucial to involve a team that understands not only your financial situation but also your personal wishes and the needs of your family.

In conclusion, undertaking estate planning will not just ensure a smooth transition of your wealth, it will guarantee it continues to provide for your loved ones well into the future. Its complexity should not be a deterrent, but rather a call to acquire the best professional guidance. Start planning today to create a reliable roadmap that nurtures your legacy and supports your family for generations to come.

Chapter 9. Teaching Financial Literacy to the Next Generations

The key to securing generational wealth lies not only in the accumulation and careful management of assets but also in the cultivation of financial intelligence among younger generations. This goes beyond simply making money — it's about understanding how to make money work for you and your descendants.

9.1. The Importance of Financial Literacy

Whether we like it or not, finance is a crucial aspect of our lives. It enables us to meet our basic needs, such as food and shelter, and enjoy luxuries that make life more pleasant. Despite its importance, many people lack an understanding of basic financial concepts, leading to poor financial decisions that affect not only their lives but also those of their descendants.

Financial literacy refers to the capability to understand and use various financial skills, including personal financial management, budgeting, and investing. Facilitating this understanding among the next generations is crucial for building and maintaining generational wealth.

9.2. Imparting Financial Wisdom Early

It's never too early to introduce your children to the world of finance. This doesn't involve drilling them on the intricacies of the stock market or tax law, but rather instilling awareness of the value of money. Here's how to do it:

9.2.1. Start with Basic Financial Terms

When children can understand basic arithmetic, start introducing financial terms such as saving, investing, earning, and spending. Explain these concepts with relatable examples, such as saving to buy a toy or investing time in learning to get better grades.

9.2.2. Explain the Value of Saving

The concept of saving is fundamental to financial literacy. Show your child how to save money using a simple piggy bank. Start by setting a savings goal, like buying a new toy. Every time money is saved, remind your child how much closer they are to their goal.

9.2.3. Demonstrate Wise Spending

Teach your children to be cautious consumers. Show them that price doesn't always equate to quality and that shopping around can net better deals. Explain the concept of budgeting, and help them develop one for their allowance.

9.3. Introducing Adolescents to Banking and Investing

As your children grow older, the concepts you teach them should evolve too. Here's how you can continue their financial education:

9.3.1. Introduce Them to Banking

Help your teenager open their first checking and savings account. Show them how to monitor their account balance, make deposits, withdraw cash, and reconcile an account statement.

9.3.2. Explore the Power of Compounding Interest

Teach them the concept of compounding interest as it's a powerful tool in wealth accumulation. Show how investing a certain amount at a young age can lead to a significant payout in the future due to compounding.

9.3.3. Encourage Investing

Explain the basics of investing. This can be done using real-world examples or simulations. Get them interested in the stock market or real estate and explain how these vehicles can aid in wealth accumulation.

9.4. Adult Children and Estate Planning

Once your offsprings have reached adulthood, they should have a solid grasp of financial principles. Now is the time they become part of your family's long-term financial plan:

9.4.1. Discuss Your Family's Financial Legacy

Discuss your family's financial goals and values. Introduce them to the concept of generational wealth, and express your desire to see it continue into the future.

9.4.2. Involvement in Estate Planning

If you have a family business, consider introducing them to it and taking them through the operations. Accompany this with discussions about succession planning and wealth transfer strategies.

9.4.3. Consult Financial Advisors Together

Involve them when consulting with your financial advisor. This can provide an in-depth look at your family's current financial state, future plans, and strategies for preserving and growing wealth.

In conclusion, by involving the younger generations in financial planning and decision making, you equip them with the necessary tools to maintain and grow the family wealth, thus ensuring the financial future of your family for generations to come. This legacy of financial literacy is the ultimate wealth you can pass onto your children, and perhaps the most enduring. With every lesson, you're ensuring the continuity of your family's financial stability and paving the way for an enduring legacy of prosperity and financial intelligence.

Chapter 10. The Role of Philanthropy in Family Legacy

For many families, their legacy isn't merely about material possessions or accumulated wealth, but also about the impact they have on the world. One powerful means for a family to etch indelible imprints of their influence is through philanthropy. Philanthropic activities are a reflection of your family's values and interests, and incorporating such endeavors into your wealth framework bolsters your family legacy.

10.1. The Intersection of Wealth and Philanthropy

Philanthropy is the act of promoting the welfare of others, typically through the donation of money, resources, or time to good causes. It is a means of directing wealth towards shaping the world in accordance with your family's values and visions. By intertwining philanthropy with wealth generation, families can create a lasting legacy which goes beyond tangible wealth.

A family's philanthropic pursuits can range from supporting a local charity to establishing nonprofit foundations, contributing to art and culture, or supporting research works and scholarships. These endeavors not only reflect your family values but also introduce the younger generation to the responsibilities that come with wealth.

10.2. Building a Philanthropic Identity

Building a philanthropic identity is a deliberate process. It begins with acknowledging the causes that resonate with your family. Identifying these causes provides direction to your philanthropy. Once these are identified, a clear mission statement for your philanthropic goals can be developed. This will guide your actions and maintain the focus of your giving.

Next comes defining what you would like to achieve with your philanthropic efforts. It's crucial to set measurable goals and objectives in order to track progress and gauge impact. This could involve improving access to education in underprivileged areas, safeguarding the environment, promoting cultural heritage, or mitigating poverty.

Involving every family member, including the younger ones, in these deliberations encourages unity and imparts the values of giving back, creating a philanthropic identity that binds everyone together and strengthens the family legacy.

10.3. Establishing a Family Foundation

One of the most effective methods through which families can channel their philanthropic efforts is by establishing a family foundation. This offers you control over your donations - where they go and how they are used. You can dictate what causes you want to support, making it an extensive provision for your philanthropic identity.

A family foundation can involve everyone in the decision-making processes, allowing younger generations to learn about wealth management, impacts of contributions, and the import of helping others. This not only fosters philanthropic values but also enables them to grasp the responsibilities accompanying wealth.

10.4. Teaching Through Philanthropy

One remarkable aspect of ingraining philanthropy into your wealth management strategy is the lesson it teaches younger generations. It not only imparts the idea of financial stewardship but also cultivates a sense of empathy and social responsibility.

Through philanthropy, children learn about wealth as not just a means for personal comfort and luxury, but also a tool for contributing to the betterment of society. It teaches them about the inequalities of the world and their privations, helping them grow into empathetic individuals who understand the significance of giving.

This active engagement in philanthropy also offers them hands-on experience with wealth management, strategic decision making, and understanding of monetary worth, preparing them for future financial stewardship.

10.5. Integrating Philanthropy into the Estate Plan

To ensure the sustainability of philanthropic endeavors, it's crucial to integrate them into your estate plan. By earmarking a notable portion of your estate for charitable causes, you ensure the continuation of your family's philanthropic activities even after you.

Such a provision sends a powerful message about your family's values to future generations, engraving the importance of philanthropy in their minds.

10.6. The Influence of Philanthropy on Family Legacy

Philanthropy plays a pivotal role in shaping your family legacy. The causes you triumph, the changes you effect, and the improvements you instill in the lives of many will become an integral part of your family history.

This philanthropic influence leaves impressions lasting generations, defining how the world perceives your family legacy. It speaks volume about your heritage, values and the effective stewardship of wealth.

In summary, the role of philanthropy in creating and strengthening family legacy is profound and manifold. It transcends the realms of wealth accumulation and management, venturing into expressing family values, instilling responsibility, unifying generations under a shared mission, and leaving a profound and lasting impact on society. Incorporating philanthropy into your wealth framework helps cement a legacy that reflects not just financial success, but integrity, empathy, and altruism as well.

Chapter 11. Adapting to Economic Challenges: A Resilient Wealth Strategy

The journey to generational wealth is not a straight path but rather a labyrinth, complete with twists, turns, and the occasional unforeseeable obstacle. Many of these obstacles present in the form of economic challenges, which possess the capacity to disrupt even the most carefully thought out plans. However, wealth creation is as much about resilience and adaptation as it is about planning and strategy. Therefore, learning to navigate economic challenges with agility and poise is a crucial skill you must develop.

11.1. Understanding Economic Challenges

The economy is akin to a living, breathing organism, constantly expanding and contracting in response to myriad factors both domestic and global. Changes in economic conditions can impact employment rates, interest rates, cost of living, and the stock market - all of which play a significant role in our individual financial standing. Adapting to these changes begins with understanding them.

For instance, consider job losses during periods of recession. These losses can directly impact family income, making survival a challenge let alone wealth accumulation. Acknowledging such risks enables us to build buffers and contingency plans to safeguard our financial health.

11.2. Building Financial Resilience

Building financial resilience is a process which involves creating safeguards to keep you and your family financially stable, regardless of external circumstances. A robust financial plan should include a diverse investment portfolio, emergency savings, and suitable insurance coverage.

To diversify investments, consider a combination of stocks, bonds, real estate, and other alternative investment paths that align with your risk tolerance. Diversification helps to mitigate risks associated with market volatility.

Emergency savings serve as a buffer during financially challenging times, whether it be sudden job loss or unexpected expenses. Ideally, you should have a sum equivalent to six months of your expenses stored in an easily accessible savings account.

Insurance, meanwhile, is instrumental in safeguarding your existing wealth. From life insurance to insuring your assets, the right insurance coverage can shield you against many unforeseen financial challenges.

11.3. Adopting a Flexible Mindset

Adaption is not solely about financial strategy; rather it extends into the realms of our attitudes and mindset. A flexible mindset will allow you to better assess changes, foresee potential challenges and adjust your plans. It's about thinking long-term, making decisions based on the future generational wealth you are aiming to accumulate, rather than immediate gains.

11.4. Staying Aware and Informed

Staying informed about global and local economic trends helps you to anticipate changes and adjust plans proactively instead of reacting hastily to financial crises. Familiarizing yourself with the predictions of renowned economists and industry leaders, along with staying updated with global news, can help identify potential economic challenges and allow you to create responsive strategies.

11.5. Proactive Debt Management

Debt is often viewed as a hindrance to wealth creation, but when strategically managed, it can be a tool for building wealth. It's important to differentiate between good debt, such as investing in education or real estate, and bad debt, such as credit card bills or high-interest loans. Having a proactive debt management plan that focuses on minimizing bad debts and responsibly managing good debts can provide a necessary boost in your journey of wealth creation and maintenance.

Understandably, economic conditions are beyond our control. However, a resilient wealth strategy, composed of an understanding of economic challenges, a diversified financial plan, a flexible mindset, remaining informed and proactive debt management, can significantly improve the odds of not just surviving, but thriving amidst these challenges. Armed with these tools, you are one step closer to realizing your goal of creating a solid foundation of generational wealth.